YOUR KNOWLEDGE HAS VALUE

AF152510

- We will publish your bachelor's and
  master's thesis, essays and papers

- Your own eBook and book -
  sold worldwide in all relevant shops

- Earn money with each sale

Upload your text at www.GRIN.com
and publish for free

Florian Kollmeier

Female Oppression in "The Bell Jar" and "A Thousand Splendid Suns"

GRIN Verlag

Bibliografische Information der Deutschen Nationalbibliothek:

Die Deutsche Bibliothek verzeichnet diese Publikation in der Deutschen National-
bibliografie; detaillierte bibliografische Daten sind im Internet über http://dnb.d-
nb.de/ abrufbar.

Imprint:

Copyright © 2013 GRIN Verlag GmbH
Druck und Bindung: Books on Demand GmbH, Norderstedt Germany
ISBN: 978-3-656-43969-1

This book at GRIN:

http://www.grin.com/en/e-book/215425/female-oppression-in-the-bell-jar-and-a-
thousand-splendid-suns

GRIN - Your knowledge has value

Der GRIN Verlag publiziert seit 1998 wissenschaftliche Arbeiten von Studenten, Hochschullehrern und anderen Akademikern als eBook und gedrucktes Buch. Die Verlagswebsite www.grin.com ist die ideale Plattform zur Veröffentlichung von Hausarbeiten, Abschlussarbeiten, wissenschaftlichen Aufsätzen, Dissertationen und Fachbüchern.

Visit us on the internet:

http://www.grin.com/

http://www.facebook.com/grincom

http://www.twitter.com/grin_com

Research Question:

'Looking at "The Bell Jar" and "A Thousand Splendid Suns", discuss the notion that the representation of female oppression in literature transcends cultural differences.'

Table of Contents

Looking at *The Bell Jar* and *A 1000 Splendid Suns* discuss the notion that the representation of female oppression in literature transcends cultural differences.

Introduction

"Women face restrictions which, on-balance, are harmful to them; they are

imposed by social structures and expectations, and even within the law; women

face them because of their status as women; and men both impose these barriers

and benefit from them."[1]

Virginia Woolf argued for female freedom, not only but particularly in literature.

It has been assumed that the situation of women in literature nowadays is equal

to that of their male counterparts and generally accepted that female oppression

is more known in developing countries such as Afghanistan. However, when

reading Sylvia Plath's novel *The Bell Jar,* it seems striking that in this

representation of an American woman's life in 1950s America, women like Esther

still suffer from oppression.

I decided to discuss two novels of different socio-cultural and political

background to show that the oppression of the female in literature is apparent in

different societies; yet it may take on different forms.

In the course of this essay I intend to develop a greater sense of how these forms

of oppression differ and how they are depicted.

---

[1] http://em-journal.com/2012/03/fryes-oppression-an-inadequate-definition-1.html accessed Jan 3rd 2013

Main Body

In Khaled Hosseini's *A Thousand Splendid Suns,* and Sylvia Plath's *The Bell Jar,* the main female characters, Esther, Laila and Mariam are alienated from their society and are very different. Mariam is born a "Harami", a bastard child in Afghanistan of the late 1950s whilst Esther grows up in the United States during the 1950s. Laila, like Mariam, grows up in Afghanistan and lives with her liberal parents in Kabul.

Cultural differences are often seen as a rationale for oppressive behaviour towards women. In *The Bell Jar,* Esther lives in the sexually liberal America of the 1950s. Although women in the West have freedom of expression, this may lead to expectations that may cause women to feel pressured to fit in. Esther experiences this pressure with her sexual life:

"When I was nineteen, pureness was the great issue. Instead of the world being divided up into Catholics and Protestants [...] I saw the world divided into people who had slept with somebody and people who hadn't." [2]

To Hosseini sexuality is not a topic of public talk as this is not something permitted in the Afghan culture. Women have to take care not to become a subject of talk regarding their sexuality their virginity.

"The reputation of a girl, especially one as pretty as you is a delicate thing"[3]

The duty of a girl to keep her virginity and the threat of sanctions of society are a way of oppressing the female, as she cannot decide freely over her sexual life. In that sense the female characters of the texts live under very different conditions regarding sexual freedom of women in their individual cultures. Laila

---

[2] *The Bell Jar* p77
[3] *A Thousand Splendid Suns* p160

and Mariam are subject to Islamic law in Afghanistan and throughout the story have to comply with the Taliban laws that begin to shape their lives whilst Esther is granted free movement and makes decisions herself. It is therefore interesting to see that many works of literature blame culture and society for the oppression of the female characters. Hosseini portrays the oppression of women as something that is part of Afghan daily life. As the oppression comes from society rather than the individual, Laila and Mariam's sufferings are to be seen as a representation of the real world.

Whilst it may appear the women are maltreated in nations without equality laws, it still is something that is conducted behind closed doors in the more developed world. The oppression of women in the West is rarely talked about; it may be equal or worse to that happening in countries such as Afghanistan.
Despite the fact that women are able to move around freely in the West, oppression is still often practised in domestic environments.
Aristotle said a wife should be as "obedient as a slave". Furthermore he views this inequality as a "natural defectiveness"[4] Although this assertion dates back to ancient Greece, it is in no means dated. Today women in the West are often expected to fulfil certain gender roles. The expectation of a woman being in the role of the mother and housewife is still very common in the Western world. Nonetheless, it is a way of society to stifle women and women find themselves not being able to fit a career and nursing a child at once.
In *The Bell Jar*, this is something Esther fears to fall into. It is this struggle for independence that eventually leads her into trying to end her life.

---

[4] http://womeninworldhistory.com/WR-12.html accessed Nov 1 2012

Esther's struggle is a representation of the author's genuine voice. Plath herself struggled for equality in her relationship with Ted Hughes. She would often take time to type up his works rather than to publish her own poetry.

In order to analyse the oppression of females in literature one has to distinguish between mental and physical oppression[5], which may take forms of abuse. Whereas in *The Bell Jar* physical abuse is not an issue as such, Esther is oppressed mentally. Unlike other girls of her age Esther does not want to be married off to a husband but rather become a writer. In that way she is different from the norm in society. This leads Esther to an inner struggle that eventually causes her to attempt suicide and she ends up in an asylum for women where she is being given shock treatments that completely stifle her creativity. These treatments were often prescribed to patients as a remedy for anxiety, hysteria and angst; the patient becoming docile. This is something Esther always feared. Therefore commonly accepted treatments are disallowing Esther to develop her own personality but make her a person suitable for society. This is an example of how Plath uses the Gothic genre to underline Esther's struggle for freedom. The representation of female oppression through the use of the Gothic genre is present throughout the history of literature as is evidenced in Brontë's *Jane Eyre,* published in 1847. Bertha is forced to live locked-up in an attic, as she is considered mad.. The eeriness around her oppression is conveyed through the use of emotive language that further settles the idea of Bertha being oppressed in the reader's mind.

In *A Doll's House,* Nora is not physically oppressed, but her husband deliberately dominates her by controlling her every move. Ibsen shows the oppression though

---

[5] http://en.wikipedia.org/wiki/Oppression accessed 2013-01-06

the use of symbolism. Helmer calls Nora his 'song bird' and his 'squirrel'[6], linguistically diminishing her and fails to treat her as a person with thoughts and ideas.

In *A Thousand Splendid Suns,* it is apparent that female oppression and abuse takes both forms. Besides being raped, Mariam also has to endure teasing from her mother, as she is a harami. More importantly however, is the fact that as the Taliban came to power in the 1980s women like Mariam and Laila have to obey newly implemented Islamic law such as not leaving the house alone and more so as they were denied the right to be educated. This shows how culture leads society to oppress women. The deliberate denial of the existence of women by restricting their right of appearing outside the house and stopping their education is a way of oppressing females and not allowing them to live an independent life.

In the *Bell Jar,* Plath chooses to write in the first person:

"I am climbing to freedom, freedom from fear, freedom from marrying the wrong person, like Buddy, just because of sex, freedom from the Florence Crittenden Homes, where all the girls go who should have been fitted out like me [...]"[7]

This is a deliberate choice of the author to create a personal tone as the reader becomes witness to Esther's innermost thoughts and feelings and therefore sympathises with her. The use of the first person is a representation of Plath's voice and hence Esther's struggles may represent Plath's struggles for independence and acceptance in her personal relationship.

---

[6] *A Doll's House* Act 1 p24
[7] *The Bell Jar* p213

Plath tells Esther's story using the Modernist stream of consciousness that was used by her personal idols, Woolf and Joyce. The use of on-going monologues and flashbacks in Esther's thought processes has the effect that the inner pressure is expressed and the reader gets a feeling of suffocation:

"I had a great yearning lately, to pay my father back for all the years of neglect, and start tending his grave. I had always been my father's favourite, and it seemed fitting I should take on a mourning my mother had never bothered with [...]"[8]

Although this technique shows Esther's feeling of being unhinged, towards the end of the novel, as she has her final breakdown, this is not used. This symbolises the power and resistance of women, but also how they eventually break under the pressure.

A Thousand Splendid Suns is not constructed in such a manner. Hosseini uses a third person narrative to tell the story. This creates distance between the reader and the characters, therefore the actions become more abstract. More wide-ranging the effect is that they seem more severe from an outsider's point of view:

"She was shaking even before his fingers worked her shirt buttons [...] She felt his eyes crawling all over her [...] Then she lifted the blanket and let her finger bleed on the sheets where they had lain together."[9]

The author highlights the women's struggle to keep society's morals and not to be seen as sinning though her loss of virginity.

Paired with the female oppression that is conveyed in the events; through violence the reader begins to sympathise with Laila and Mariam. The abstraction

---

[8] *The Bell Jar* p159
[9] *A Thousand Splendid Suns* p214

of the representation of the oppression of women in *A Thousand Splendid Suns*
has the effect that the readers becomes complicit with the oppression and shifts
the focus onto society as a whole rather than just Mariam and Laila.

To strengthen this effect, and to evoke an emotional response from the reader,
Hosseini uses very descriptive language:

"Through chattering teeth she asked him to turn out the light"[10]

Words such as "chattering" along with precise descriptions of the surroundings
enable the reader to vividly picture the scene.

In order to talk about female oppression in *A Thousand Splendid Suns,* Hosseini
uses two contrasting characters. From an early age, Mariam is being told to
endure and suffer. This is something that is alien to Laila. Whilst Mariam endures
torture and rape, Laila sees the injustice and takes courage to fight it. Despite
showing oppression of females, this character sketch shows the immense power
of women.

"The girl lunged at him. She grabbed his arm with both hands and tried to drag

him down, but she could not do more than dangle from it. She did succeed in

slowing Rasheed's progress toward Mariam."[11]

The power of Mariam's endurance is remarkable, even when Rasheed has sex
with her she does not fight back:

"The pain was sudden and astonishing. Her eyes sprang open. She sucked air

through her teeth and bit on the knuckle of her thumb."[12]

---

[10] *A Thousand Splendid Suns* p214
[11] *A Thousand Splendid Suns* p235
[12] *A Thousand Splendid Suns* p76

It is only when Mariam and Laila become close friends that Mariam gives up her endurance and begins to fight for her own freedom. This development becomes important when Mariam and Laila try to flee from Rasheed.

When investigating why Mariam endures, contrast between Laila and Mariam becomes significant. Laila grows up with liberal parents whereas Nana brings Mariam up with the knowledge of being a harami and her father being a despicable man. Mariam's relationship to her father is shaped by Jalil not wanting to see Mariam and Nana's descriptions. Hence Mariam is bound to view men as cruel creatures. Laila however grows up under different circumstances. She has a close relationship with her father, who supports her and believes that she must be educated. This shows how little female oppression in literature has to do with culture. It is more something practised individually.

Due to changing political conflicts throughout *A Thousand Splendid Sun's* temporal narrative, the female characters are forced to behave as they are told. Rasheed forces his wives to wear the burka when leaving the house. This is a direct violation of their freedom to interact with others. In contrast to *The Bell Jar,* it is interesting to see that Esther who has freedom to make decisions still falls into madness and into self-hatred. This suggests that freedom in the West is of a shallow kind that does not go deep enough to fight female oppression.

Esther seemingly has everything Laila and Mariam struggle for, such as the freedom to chose whom to love, she still struggles to live her life, as she wants to live it. Esther is different to other girls of her age in that she wants to be independent and chose her own path. In this sense Esther's mother becomes a role model for her daughter as she managed to sustain the family after the father's death. Despite the fact that her mother is a strong woman in a patriarchal society,

Esther finds fault in her mother as she enslaved herself to Esther's father and did not pursue her own goals. Besides being the strong mother when the father dies, Esther's mother still upholds the importance of her daughter keeping her virginity on Esther who considers this an out dated idea.

Although Esther admires and respects her mother, she still rejects her ways of sustaining the family by doing secretarial work.

"My own mother wasn't much help. [...] She was always on to me to learn

shorthand after college so I had a practical skill as well as a college degree."[13]

Esther finds it hard to accept this suggestion; being a secretary was the embodiment of a woman's job at the time. Esther realises that it is not creative and furthermore she is reminded of her mother conducting the father's research and planning his publications.

As Sibylle Duda argues in *Wahnsinns Frauen,* there is no such thing as a mentally healthy woman for society.

" [...] A woman is only considered normal, if she accepts her role in society and

does not fight the boundaries of her position. Should she break those, she is said

to be mad or made mad. "[14]

Therefore the question arises whether or not freedom is an illusive quality. How free is a person who is physically and mentally bullied in the West despite the fact that they possess freedom?

Throughout history the diagnosis of madness in a woman was a way they could be oppressed. Women such as Camille Claudel[15] were sent to asylums where they

---

[13] *The Bell Jar* p36
[14] *Wahnsinns Frauen* p9

underwent treatments to make them accept the limits society placed upon them.
It is interesting to see that women with creative minds often worked for their
husbands. Only through them was it possible for their husbands to achieve great
success. This view is supported by Germaine Greer:

"The house wife is an unpaid employee in her husband's house in return for

being a permanent employee."[16]

Greer relates the oppression of women to their status in marriage and their
position in the home. Greer gets support for this from evidence from Sylvia Plath's
Journals where she would comment that she would help her husband complete
his work rather than her own. Through keeping women so dependent on their
partner, they would become unable to lead their own working lives. The level of
oppression of the female transcends the boundaries of the house and even
reaches psychotherapy where it has been thought that hysteria was a female
disorder that would be cured by removing the uterus.

With regards to *The Bell Jar* and *A Thousand Splendid Suns,* the search for freedom
is an unobtainable hope while oppression still exists. Is freedom necessary for the
pursuit of happiness?

In order to discuss this, it appears essential to define female freedom as the right
to self-determination.

Despite being a violation against women's freedom to choose how to dress, in
A Thousand Splendid Suns, the burka is a symbol for a shield against the evaluative
eyes of society.

---

[15] French sculptor and artist
[16] Germaine Greer
http://www.brainyquote.com/quotes/quotes/g/germainegr391026.html
accessed 2012-11-02

In *The Bell Jar* Esther is confronted with the judgement by society. She is free to wear whatever she desires but seems to be under pressure to fulfil the expectations of society. Esther is constantly obsessed with trying to fit into society, so she buys expensive clothes she does not even like in order to gain approval. This shows how Esther experiences the oppression despite living in a society that is seen as liberal.

Regardless of the differences in the way the women in *A Thousand Splendid Suns* and *The Bell Jar* are experiencing oppression, they are denied the right to determine who they are and hence have no freedom.

Since the oppression of the female characters is present in both *A Thousand Splendid Suns* and *The Bell Jar,* it seems that oppression of females in literature is not primarily an issue of cultural differences but rather a general gender conflict. In *A Thousand Splendid Suns,* the narrative style adds greatly to support the gender conflict in the relationships within the novel. By choosing to write about this inequality on the domestic level, Hosseini manages to make it seem as if all the Afghan women were in a similar situation to Rasheed's wives. The use of the third person further allows him to show his characters responding to the changing political situation around them and allows the reader to take an omniscient view.

"Two and a half years later Mariam awoke on the morning of September 27 to the sounds of shouting, whistling, firecrackers and music [...] Mariam had first heard of the Taliban two years before [...] they were a guerrilla force he said [...]" [17] Social class is a theme that is important in the beginning of *A Thousand Splendid Suns.* Mariam is a harami because she is born out of wedlock and her father

---

[17] *A Thousand Splendid Suns* p266

refuses to acknowledge her. This puts her at the very bottom of society. Nana constantly reminds her daughter of her lowly status:

"This is my reward for everything I have endured. An heirloom-breaking clumsy little harami. [...] Nana meant than a harami was an unwanted thing; that she, Mariam was an illegitimate person [...]"[18]

In spite of the fact that being called a harami is not against women, this title shapes Mariam's life prospects. As society does not view a harami as a legitimate person they do not have any rights. Due to her upbringing on the isolated kolba, Mariam does not know how much her lowly status in Afghan society will affect her life later on. When Mariam finds out that her mother committed suicide, Jalil tries his best to remove Mariam from his house. She is forced into a marriage with the Kabuli shoemaker Rasheed.

Forced marriages are a common way to oppress women and to remove women from society. Just like Rasheed's marriages, these forced arrangements often take on domestic violence, and gender stereotypes regardless of the culture of the subjects. After Mariam moves in with Rasheed he explains her duties and responsibilities:

"I expect you to start behaving like a wife. Fahmidi? Is that understood?"[19]

As Mariam has no education, there does not seem to be an alternative for her apart from marrying Rasheed. This shows the inequality of women from the earliest age. Girls are seen as less worthy than boys and are often disadvantaged and do not attend school.

---

[18]*A Thousand Splendid Suns* p4
[19] *A Thousand Splendid Suns* p63

"After she gave Rasheed the news about the baby, he had immediately prayed for it to be a boy"[20]

This puts girls at a disadvantage from the beginning of their lives. The banning of women from education hinders Mariam's ability to become independent. The phenomenon of women being trapped in marriages is not something exclusive to Afghan society.

In Ibsen's *A Doll's House* a similar conflict is described although the conditions under which females lived in Norway during the 19th century were very different to Afghanistan in *A Thousand Splendid Suns.*

Nora struggles for her own identity and freedom. Her husband oppresses her and this is conveyed through various pet names. Towards the end of the play, when Nora decides to leave her husband Helmer, the audience is aware that she is walking into a future full of uncertainties.

To further support the notion of women being disadvantaged in marriages and relationships is the idea of polygamy. After the death of Laila's parents she has no choice but to marry Rasheed despite Mariam's protesting, Rasheed takes Laila as his second wife. Although Laila does not want to marry Rasheed she is aware that she would face life on the dangerous streets of Kabul and further fears being outcast from society as she is bearing Tariq's child.

As the husband to two wives, Rasheed has the freedom to visit them whenever he likes. His freedom to do so contrasts with Laila and Mariam rights. It is legitimate for Rasheed to use them regardless of their feelings.

The conflict of freedom in marriages represented in *A Doll's House* and

---

[20] *A Thousand Splendid Suns* p222

A Thousand Splendid Suns is shown as symbolic condescension. Nora suffers from not being taken seriously and undermined by Helmer's pet names. Mariam and Laila live in a polygamist marriage and have little say over their circumstances. The fear of the oppression marriage may bring is something that is central to Esther's conflict in *The Bell Jar*.

During the post war years of the 1950s there was an emerging movement of emancipation and the fight for gender equality. [21] Esther is experiencing these developments first hand. She observes her mother advising her to learn shorthand so she would have a practical skill whilst at the same time girls like Doreen have affairs and are sexually open.

In her publication, *Feminine Mystique,* Betty Friedman draws up the concept of the feminine mystique, which goes against the role of women belonging behind the stove. In relation to Esther, Friedman states that it is permitted for Buddy to have several girlfriends whereas that is not something that would be allowed for a woman.

Esther's struggle for freedom is pictured throughout the novel using symbolism and foreshadowing:

"The bell jar hung, suspended, a few feet above my head. I was open to the circulating air."[22]

Plath uses a bell jar to describe the feelings of suffocation and oppression Esther lives through. It is repeated throughout the text and indicates the feelings of the narrator. This is important, as Esther appears to be an unreliable narrator. This is

---

[21] Vanessa Martins Lamb, *The 1950s and 1960s and the American woman* http://dumas.ccsd.cnrs.fr/docs/00/68/08/21/PDF/V_Martins_Lamb_-_Civi_2011.pdf
[22] *The Bell Jar* p206

shown in the text through her madness and the sudden shifts of moods that mirror her inner confusion.

Looking at *A Thousand Splendid Suns* and *The Bell Jar* from a non-contextual viewpoint it becomes apparent that both discuss female oppression. One would think that a woman would know best about this matter, however it seems cynical that *A Thousand Splendid Suns* is written by a man. Indeed this may be seen as an act of oppression. In *The Bell Jar*, Plath uses Esther to develop a poetic self. Many of the things Esther goes through have been taken directly from Plath's life; for example Esther and Plath share a beekeeping father.

Although both texts are of a fictional kind they convey the message of female oppression using narrative techniques and direct examples.

Conclusion

Through the precise descriptions of oppression and the struggles for freedom of Esther, Mariam and Laila, both Plath and Hosseini are able to show that female oppression in literature transcends differences in culture. The effects of society are displayed using contrasting reactions of the main characters. Whilst Mariam endures her oppression at first, Laila takes courage for her rights and Esther falls into madness. In *The Bell Jar*, the bell jar becomes a symbol for Esther's struggle for acceptance and freedom.

Both Hosseini and Plath use stylistic and symbolic devices to underlay their arguments.

The adaptation of an object standing for Esther's oppression in *The Bell Jar* is something also found in Ibsen's *A Doll's House.* Here the doll's house shrinks the actions to a much smaller scale and Nora represents the diminution of all women.

In the two texts under discussion the only differences in the representation of female oppression are due to the dominant factors at play in both contexts. The world of 1950's America and 1950s to contemporary Afghanistan still show the undermining of women and lack of self-determination still prevalent in all male dominated societies in spite of their obvious differences of how the women are oppressed.

Bibliography

Curriculum, W. i. (1996-2012, 1 1). *Women In World History*. Retrieved November 1, 2012, from Women's Rights From Past To Present: http://womeninworldhistory.com/WR-12.html

Duda, S. (1994). *Wahnsinns Frauen.* Frankfurt am Main: Suhrkamp.

Gill, J. (2006). *The Cambridge Companion To Sylvia Plath.* Cambridge: Cambridge University Press.

Gillingham, E. (2012, March 1). *EM-Journal*. Retrieved January 9, 2013, from Frye's Oppression: An Inadequate Definition: http://em-journal.com/2012/03/fryes-oppression-an-inadequate-definition-1.html

Hosseini, K. (2008). *A Thousand Splendid Suns.* London: Bloomsbury.

Ibsen, H. (1985). *A Doll's House.* London: Methuen Drama.

Lamb, V. M. (2011, June 1). *http://dumas.ccsd.cnrs.fr.* Retrieved January 8, 2013, from The 1950's and 1960's and the American Woman: the transition from the "housewife" to the feminist : http://dumas.ccsd.cnrs.fr/docs/00/68/08/21/PDF/V_Martins_Lamb_-_Civi_2011.pdf

Network, B. R. (2001-2013, January 1). *Brainy Quote*. Retrieved November 2, 2012, from The wife is an unpaid... at Brainy Quote: http://www.brainyquote.com/quotes/quotes/g/germainegr391026.html

Plath, S. (1963). *The Bell Jar.* London: Faber and Faber.

Woolf, V. (1929). *A Room Of One's Own.* Orlando: Harcourt Brace & Company.